The Life and Times of

BETSY ROSS

Mitchell Lane
PUBLISHERS

P.O. Box 196 · Hockessin, Delaware 19707

Titles in the Series

The Life and Times of

BETSY ROSS

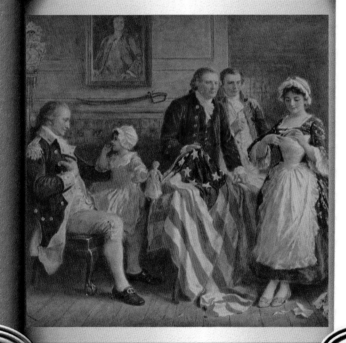

Susan Sales Harkins and
William H. Harkins

Printing   2   3   4   5   6   7   8   9

Library of Congress Cataloging-in-Publication Data
Harkins, Susan Sales.
    The life and times of Betsy Ross / by Susan Sales Harkins and William H. Harkins.
        p. cm. — (Profiles in American history)
    Includes bibliographical references and index.
    ISBN 1-58415-446-2 (library bound : alk. paper)
    1. Ross, Betsy, 1752–1836—Juvenile literature. 2. Revolutionaries—United States—Biography—Juvenile literature. 3. United States—History—Revolution, 1775–1783—Flags—Juvenile literature. 4. Flags—United States—History—18th century—Juvenile literature. I. Harkins, William H. II. Title. III. Series.
E302.6.R77H37 2006
973.3′092—dc22   2005028495

ISBN-13: 9781584154464

ABOUT THE AUTHORS: Susan and William Harkins live in Kentucky, where they enjoy writing together for children. Susan has written many books for adults and children. William is a history buff. In addition to writing, he is a member of the Air National Guard.

PHOTO CREDITS: Cover, pp. 1, 3, 6, 16, 17, 20, 24, 26, 28, 30, 38, 40—Library of Congress.

Profiles in American History

Contents

*For Your Information

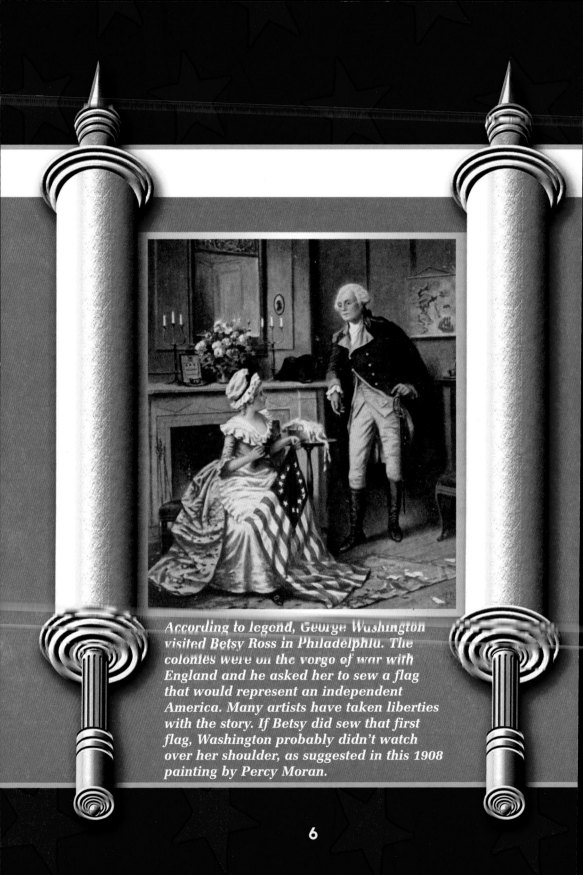

According to legend, George Washington visited Betsy Ross in Philadelphia. The colonies were on the verge of war with England and he asked her to sew a flag that would represent an independent America. Many artists have taken liberties with the story. If Betsy did sew that first flag, Washington probably didn't watch over her shoulder, as suggested in this 1908 painting by Percy Moran.

CHAPTER 1

The Legend of Betsy Ross

The spring of 1776 wafts over New England with its usual sweet smells and mild breezes, but Philadelphians have no time to notice. The militiamen that fill the streets are a new and unnerving sight. Young men, away from home for the first time, loiter in the streets waiting for General George Washington to call them to battle. The sight of so many soldiers is a constant reminder to everyone that war is coming to Philadelphia.

Not everyone is a Patriot, but everyone dreads going to war. Tempers are high. A clerk stops arguing with a customer just long enough to cheer a group of soldiers in the street. Mothers burn dinner and are impatient with their children. Plaintive wives watch their husbands leave home for drills. The men, more used to handling hammers than rifles, try to reassure their wives.

On Arch Street, Betsy Ross arranges embroidered pillows and other fine needlework in her shop's front window. She watches as a young boy pelts a horse with a rock. The horse complains loudly and its rider struggles to calm the scared beast.

Betsy grimaces as the boy's mother boxes his ears. Just ahead a few steps, the boy's father stops to chastise both his wife and his son. He is too busy for nonsense, he shouts.

All the while, people file past Betsy's window, paying no attention to her or the family drama outside her shop. Everyone is preoccupied with more important matters. With the war still ahead of them, they believe that anticipating the coming struggle is the hardest part of the ordeal. In the coming winter, under the occupation of the British, they'll realize just how wrong they were. Philadelphians will suffer serious hardships before the war is over.

While her city waits, Betsy mourns. Her beloved husband, John Ross, died just months before while guarding a Patriot munitions stash. Losing John to the war seems a high price to pay for independence.

While Betsy sews, she remembers her life with John. They shared a lot, even their livelihood. Betsy is struggling to keep their small upholstery shop open. When John died, she replaced their shop sign with a simpler one that read: Elizabeth Ross Upholsterer.

While the colonies challenge England for independence, she tries to remain self-sufficient. Business is slow because of the war; supplies are often hard to come by. Her parents want her to close her shop and move home. Betsy is determined to stay in the home she made with John.

One morning in early June, three gentlemen visit Betsy at her shop. She lays aside her work to greet Colonel George Ross, her late husband's uncle, and General George Washington. Betsy and John had chatted with the famous general at Christ Church during his visits to Philadelphia. The pew in which the Rosses sat was next to the general's. Betsy was honored when he asked her to embroider ruffles for some of his shirts. She admired him as a gentleman and as a Patriot.

After introducing a third gentleman, Robert Morris, her husband's uncle explains their visit. Congress has yet to declare independence, he says, but they all know it is coming. Acting in secret, they want to be ready for that day. Colonel Ross knows that Betsy sympathizes with the Patriots.

"Betsy, would you be willing to sew a flag for the united colonies?" he asks.

Betsy knows she can't fight, but she can sew. "I have never made a flag before, but I will try," she replies.

After settling her guests in the back parlor, Betsy looks over a sketch that General Washington hands her: thirteen white six-point stars on a field of dark blue atop alternating red and white stripes. Betsy's adept eyes catch two flaws.

"The flag should be longer to catch the wind so it will wave better," she explains to the committee. "Also, a five-point star is more balanced than your six-point star."

General Washington believes that the five-point star will be too difficult to make.

Betsy folds a piece of paper several times; it takes her just a few seconds. Then, the committee watches as she makes one quick snip with her scissors and unfolds a perfect five-point star.[1] The committee members are overjoyed to have found such a talented seamstress. General Washington quickly revises his sketch to include Betsy's suggestions.

Early the next morning, Betsy visits the wharf and boards one of Mr. Morris's ships. There, a clerk removes an old flag from a chest and hands it to Betsy. She's to study the techniques used to make the flag. He also gives her a watercolor painted quickly the night before at General Washington's special request. The painting is of a flag—the general's flag with her changes.

Back in her small shop, Betsy sews almost nonstop for several days. As she skillfully sews each stitch, she begins to feel hopeful for the first time in months. Each stitch replaces a bit of her sorrow with hope.

With her head bent over her work and her fingers flying, she admires the colors and the design. Mostly, she admires the stars. There are thirteen of them, one for each American colony. Under this new flag—*her* flag—all thirteen colonies will be united. What a privilege and an honor to be a part of her country's independence.

Although Betsy doesn't know it, just a few streets away, another Patriot is giving his all for the cause. As Betsy sews the nation's first flag, Thomas Jefferson drafts the nation's Declaration of Independence.

A few days after the meeting in Betsy's parlor, the committee raises her flag on one of Morris's ships. Bystanders burst into applause at the sight of the waving flag—they love Betsy's Stars and Stripes.

The next day, Colonel Ross startles Betsy as he rushes through her front door.

"Betsy! The committee approved your flag!"

Betsy barely has time to consider the news before he clasps her hands and insists that she must put everything else aside. She must make more flags.

Betsy is overjoyed, but also overwhelmed. She doesn't have the money to buy materials, but she mustn't complain to the colonel about that. Silently, she resolves to purchase what she can and to be grateful for whatever happens.

Later that same day, Colonel Ross returns to Betsy's shop. He apologizes for being so inconsiderate earlier. Only after leaving the shop did he realize that Betsy couldn't possibly purchase the materials. He hands her a one-hundred-pound note for supplies and tells her to come to him when she needs more.

Suddenly, Betsy no longer sees her future veiled through grief. She sees the potential of a new nation, and she's relieved to have plenty of work to get her through the lean days of the war. She sits down and cries quietly to herself from joy and relief, but not for long—she has too much work to do.

Patriots all over the colonies gave what they could to the cause for independence. Some gave food and supplies. Some gave their lives. Betsy gave the new nation its flag. It's easy to imagine that sewing the nation's first flag helped to heal Betsy's broken heart. The Stars and Stripes still flies today as the most sacred of our American traditions and the symbol of hope and freedom around the world.

Christ Church, the Nation's Church

Christ Church

Although Betsy was raised as a Quaker, she attended Christ Church in Philadelphia with her husband, John Ross. Many refer to Christ Church as the Nation's Church because so many of the founding fathers, such as George and Martha Washington and Benjamin Franklin, worshiped there. The church's congregation included fifteen signers of the Declaration of Independence.

The church was established in 1695, when an Anglican (Church of England) congregation built a small wooden church. It was the first Anglican parish in Philadelphia. In 1697, All Hallow's Church Barking-by-the Tower, in London, sent the baptismal font where William Penn was baptized. (The font is still in service.) Thirty years later, in 1727, construction began on a much larger building. It took almost twenty years, until 1744, to complete it.

The bell steeple remained unfinished until 1754, when Benjamin Franklin arranged a lottery to raise some money. He used the funds to finish the tower. Interestingly, the Whitechapel foundry in England that cast the Liberty Bell also cast the bells for Christ Church. The church paid ringers nineteen pounds a year to ring the bells every Sunday and on Christmas, New Year's Day, Easter, and Whitsuntide (May 29 and November 5). Sponsors could pay to have the bells rung on special occasions, at a cost of thirty shillings.[2]

George Washington and the entire Continental Congress prayed at Christ Church before deciding to declare independence from England. On July 8, 1776, the church bells rang to announce the first public reading of the Declaration of Independence. Months later, Patriots removed the bells from Christ Church along with the Liberty Bell from Independence Hall. The bells remained hidden in Old Zion Reformed Church in Allentown during the British invasion of Philadelphia. They were returned in August of 1778.

Today, Christ Church is still a fully functional church with an Episcopalian parish. Congress designated the church as a National Shrine in 1950.[3]

For Your Information

Betsy was raised a Quaker and, as such, she wore the same style and color dress as all other Quaker women. Men wore the same basic suit as well. Rich Quakers probably had their clothing made of finer materials, such as silk. However, Quakers as a rule did not embellish their clothing with embroidery or jewelry.

CHAPTER
2

A Colonial Quaker

On New Year's Day, 1752, the Griscom family of Philadelphia, Pennsylvania, welcomed their ninth child, Elizabeth, into their family. As is the custom with Quakers, soon after the birth, her family probably took part in a naming service known as nomination.

Quaker parents, traditionally, put a lot of thought into choosing names for their children. To honor both sets of grandparents, they name their eldest son after the mother's father and their eldest daughter after her father's mother. They often rely on the Bible for other favorites, such as Elizabeth.

Family members, neighbors, and friends probably gathered to certify her name at a Meeting, which is what Quakers call their worship service. This is the Quaker way of introducing new babies into their community. Samuel and Rebecca Griscom would have presented Betsy, as they called her, to the congregation. Someone would then enter her name in the Meeting's register. Afterward, Betsy would be an official member of the Quaker community. Everyone in Betsy's family and their Quaker community would have attended.

Betsy was born during an amazing time in history. She was just six months old when Benjamin Franklin flew his famous

electricity-catching kite. A few months later, Philadelphians hung the Liberty Bell in the belfry tower that Betsy's father helped to build.

Despite the extraordinary changes occurring in the colonies, Betsy's childhood was typical in many ways, but she did have a few advantages. Betsy attended school when most girls didn't receive an education beyond what they learned at home. Her parents taught her to be an independent thinker and to express her opinions in all matters. Most women of that era didn't have the privilege of free expression. Betsy learned a trade, which she practiced almost her entire life. Most girls grew up to be mothers and homemakers; few girls learned a trade or worked outside their homes, even after they married.

Most of Betsy's day-to-day activities were similar to those of other colonial children. She helped her mother with household chores, such as carrying water and firewood. She learned to keep a clean and orderly home. In quiet moments, the older women in her family taught her how to sew.

It's easy to imagine Betsy's family gathering in the evening. Betsy would sit near the fire or a lantern, head bent over her needlework. She would work diligently, stopping only to take her turn at reading the Bible or to laugh at a younger child playing on a wooden rocking horse. Occasionally her mother and older sisters would stop their own needlework to guide Betsy's hands.

First Days (Sundays) were quiet days for Quakers. Betsy's family attended Meeting and then spent the day praying and reading from the Bible. Quakers also had Meeting on Fifth Day (Thursday), but they spent the rest of that day as any other day—doing chores, attending school, and so on.

On summer days, Betsy's family often left their hot house to enjoy a picnic. It's likely that Betsy played hopscotch and leap frog, jumped rope, and skipped. She probably knew how to fly a kite and enjoyed ice-skating with her brothers and sisters during the cold winter months.

The foundation of Betsy's life was her Quaker religion. Quakers are passive and simple-living, but they're independent. They place equal value on men and women. As such, women are free to speak their minds on all matters. Betsy's father, most likely, treated her mother with respect and kindness.

Quakers are pacifists. That means they don't use violence or force in their relationships. Nor do they support war for any reason. Betsy's parents were probably mild-mannered but firm with their children. They would have encouraged Betsy to be independent, to respect her elders, and to honor the Quaker beliefs.

Colonial Quakers dressed plainly. Betsy wore the same style dress as every other girl and woman in her Quaker community. The floor-length dress was made of gray wool or silk. The pleated skirt was full and gathered at the waist. A white apron covered the skirt, and a white linen collar adorned the neck. The same linen edged the bottom of each elbow-length sleeve. Ribbon laced up a white stomacher. Even as a young child, Betsy would have worn a simple but crisp bonnet.

As Quakers, Betsy's parents educated both their boys and their girls. Betsy started school at age six in the home of fellow Quaker Rebecca Jones.

Betsy's father was a carpenter and builder. The Griscoms weren't wealthy, but Samuel Griscom provided well for his family. Philadelphia was growing, and Samuel's skills were always in demand.

Samuel helped to build the Friends Meeting House where his family worshiped. (Quakers often referred to themselves as Friends.) He also worked on the addition of a belfry tower to the Pennsylvania State House. Today, we know this building as Independence Hall. (For a few decades, the Liberty Bell hung in this tower.)

Betsy had the additional advantage of living in the largest and most diverse city in the colonies. Philadelphia was the second largest English-speaking city in the entire world—second only to London, England.

As Betsy walked or rode through the busy and noisy streets of Philadelphia, she passed many homes and buildings that her father had built. She probably heard many different accents and languages; the town was full of immigrants from Wales, Ireland, Holland, Germany, and Scotland. She surely passed a number of

Betsy attended Quaker meetings at Friends Meeting House on Arch Street in Philadelphia, Pennsylvania. Her father helped to build the meetinghouse.

non-Quaker churches. Pennsylvania allowed its citizens to practice the religion of their choice. Baptists, Presbyterians, Catholics, and Quakers called Philadelphia home. It's likely that Betsy saw African slaves on the streets. (Quakers rejected slavery.)

Although most Philadelphians lived in neighborhoods segregated by nationality or religion, the presence of so many different groups reduced social problems. The colonial government of Pennsylvania didn't discriminate in the name of religion or nationality. In contrast, life outside Pennsylvania could be hard for Quakers.

It's likely that Betsy's parents and teachers told her the story of Mary Dyer, a Quaker martyr. The Boston authorities hanged her on June 1, 1660, for challenging their ban against Quakers. Twice, the Boston authorities made her leave Boston for being a Quaker. The third time she returned to Boston, they tried her, convicted her, and sentenced her to hang. Eventually they set her free but warned her not to return. When she did, they showed her no mercy. On the morning of June 1, soldiers marched Mary to

Mary Dyer, a Quaker martyr, was hanged in Boston in 1660. Boston forbid Quakers in the city but Mary was eager to convert non-Quakers. She returned every time they banished her. Betsy never faced that type of discrimination as a Quaker in Pennsylvania.

the gallows. Unlike before, no reprieve came, and the citizens of Boston watched Mary hang until she was dead.[1]

As Betsy grew older in a safe Philadelphia, her responsibilities grew. At home, she learned to cook, to make candles and soap, to spin wool, and to weave cloth. Eventually, she outgrew Mrs. Jones's school and began to attend the Friends Public School. There, Betsy spent several hours a day studying. She studied the basics: reading, writing, and arithmetic. During the last hour of each day, Betsy worked to perfect her needleworking skills.

At the Friends Public School, Betsy met Susan Claypoole, who became her best and lifelong friend. Although Quakers ran the school, many wealthy non-Quaker families sent their children there. Most likely, Betsy associated with non-Quakers for the first time in her life.

Betsy's life changed in 1764 when she left school to apprentice to a Quaker upholsterer. She worked in John Webster's shop all day to learn the trade. No one knows whether her parents encouraged her to become an apprentice or whether she sought the position herself. Most likely, her father secured the spot for her, but it isn't likely that he would have forced her into the trade if she hadn't been agreeable. That wasn't the Quaker way. We do know that by age twelve, Betsy was already an accomplished seamstress,[2] so the shop was a good fit for her.

Under Mr. Webster's tutelage, Betsy learned a skill that served her well her entire life. However, the shop changed her life in another big way—in a way no one had counted on. While apprenticing for Mr. Webster, Betsy fell in love with John Ross, another apprentice at the shop. The two eventually married, and it was through her husband's uncle, Colonel George Ross, that Betsy—as tradition holds—came to sew America's first flag.

More About Quakers

In seventeenth-century America, colonists were not free to practice any religion they chose. On the contrary, most colonies had an established religion. Not attending the right church was enough to get a person a day in the stocks in most communities.

George Fox

At that time, *religious freedom* meant that a colony didn't have to follow the Church of England (Anglican Church) or the Catholic Pope.

George Fox was an English commoner who challenged the contemporary Anglican and Catholic churches. He didn't set out to create a new religion, but eventually he founded the Religious Society of Friends, also known as Quakers. The basic tenets of this Christian-based sect follow:

- Religion should not oppress or discriminate based on race, sex, or class.
- Everyone is capable of having a personal relationship with God, without the intervention or the permission of clergy.
- Men and women are equal in all matters, including religion. Respect is given equally to all. Persons of authority are equal to everyone else.
- Worship services, known as Meetings, are silent until a Friend feels compelled to speak.
- War is unacceptable. Quakers do not support or participate in war.
- Physical force or mental coercion shall not be used to persuade another.
- Rituals are forbidden.
- No statement of belief or creed is followed.
- No Quaker may swear allegiance to any individual.
- No Quaker may take or make oaths.
- Tithing is not practiced, although each community does support a meetinghouse.
- There is no marriage ceremony. To be married, a man and woman simply promise to love one another before witnesses.

Betsy's Quaker upbringing instilled in her a sense of resolve, personal value, and purpose. Flag making aside, she was an independent and courageous woman—for any time. She stood strong in her beliefs and faced uncertain times with courage and hope.

For Your Information

Tradition tells us that Betsy Ross lived at this house, 239 Arch Street in Philadelphia, Pennsylvania, when she sewed the first Stars and Stripes flag. When Betsy lived there, the address was 89 Arch Street. Some claim she never lived there, but the evidence seems to prove that she did. This photo was taken in 1903, when only two rooms were open to the public. In 1937, the entire house was renovated as a museum.

CHAPTER 3

Betsy and the Colonies Come of Age

By the end of 1773, relations between the colonies and England were tense. The Tea Act of 1773 outraged the colonists. This act allowed the British East India Company to sell tea in the colonies without paying the import tax that the colonists paid. Colonists called for a boycott against English tea, but they still hoped to reconcile with England.

Betsy was waging her own personal battle. Her parents opposed her marriage to John Ross. Quakers don't marry outside the faith, and John Ross belonged to the Church of England.

Tradition tells us that on November 4, 1773, Betsy left her family and her Quaker community to elope with John Ross. Under the cover of darkness, the couple sailed a small boat across the Delaware River to Gloucester, New Jersey. A justice of the peace married the couple at Hugg's Tavern.

Betsy's Quaker community read her out of Meeting on May 24, 1774. That action severed Betsy from her Quaker roots. For Betsy, there would be no reconciliation with the Quakers.[1]

Betsy joined John's church, which had to be a big change for her. The congregation sang and a minister preached long, passionate sermons from the pulpit. Betsy was used to silent worship services in the Quaker fashion.

Both Betsy and John continued to work for John Webster in his upholstery business, but now they were paid craftsmen. They hoped to save enough money to open their own shop someday.

The young couple had been married only a short time when news of the Boston Tea Party reached Philadelphia. On December 16, 1773, Boston Patriots, disguised as Mohawk Indians, ran through the streets to the harbor. The rioters boarded tea ships anchored in the harbor and tossed their cargoes—342 chests of tea—into the water.

On December 27, the excitement reached Philadelphia. A group of 8,000 angry Philadelphians met the *Polly* (a tea ship) at the dock. The captain turned the ship around and left the port. Betsy and John were Patriots, so it is possible that they stood on the crowded dock and watched as the *Polly* sailed away.

In retaliation against the Boston colonists, Parliament passed the Coercive Acts (called the Intolerable Acts in the colonies). British troops occupied Boston. They allowed ships to unload only essential goods, such as medicine and ammunition for the troops. British officers lived anywhere they liked, including in the private homes of Boston's wealthier citizens.

In response to the occupation of Boston, Patriots from all over the colonies converged on Philadelphia for the First Continental Congress. Although this historic meeting took place in secrecy, the delegates didn't try very hard to hide their presence or their sentiments. When the delegates arrived that first morning at New Tavern, they cheered loudly. As a group, they walked through the streets to Carpenters' Hall, a building Betsy's father helped to build. Once inside, they shouted and applauded. Philadelphians heard the commotion and saw the men about town. The citizens probably suspected the group's purpose.

From September 5 to October 12 of 1774, the delegates debated. Some thought the boycott would force England to listen to their complaints. Others were ready to declare independence. One thing they could all agree upon—they must do something to free Boston.

Few were ready to go to war with England, so the delegates took a nonaggressive approach. They voted to continue the boycott, and they sent a bill of rights to the king. John Adams and Henry Lee drafted the bill, but King George refused to read it.

Conditions in Boston and throughout Massachusetts grew worse. Patriots stocked military supplies outside Boston in a village named Concord. The British moved to capture the supplies. On April 19, 1775, seventy minutemen tried to stop seven hundred British troops at Lexington. The British killed only eight colonists before marching to Concord, where they met thousands of minutemen. Over three hundred British soldiers died in that battle.

It didn't take long for Philadelphians to get the news. Like it or not, they were at war with England.

Delegates of the Second Continental Congress met that year from May to July. Congress created a Continental Army and appointed George Washington its commander in chief. Before General Washington could join his troops, Massachusetts militiamen engaged the British at Bunker Hill—twice.

General Washington left while Congress was still in session, on June 21, 1775. He rode through streets of cheering Patriots as he headed for Boston. Betsy and John probably cheered him too as he marched out of Philadelphia.

That same year, Betsy and John moved to a small brick house on Arch Street. They opened a shop on the first floor, and they lived on the second floor. Starting a new business at the beginning of a war probably wasn't an easy task, but they were determined to make it on their own.

Despite the war, or perhaps because of the war, Philadelphia was a busy place. War brought lots of business to town. Betsy and John worked six days a week in their new shop. They upholstered furniture and made tablecloths, bed curtains, and drapes.

Betsy joined a group that called themselves The Fighting Quakers. They were Quaker Patriots who had been read out of Meeting for supporting the war. Betsy was able to join, too, since the Quakers had read her out of Meeting months earlier. John joined the militia and helped guard Philadelphia and a large stash of munitions.

After liberating Boston, General Washington raised America's first flag over Boston. It was January 1, 1776. The Continental

During the Second Continental Congress in 1775, the delegates put George Washington (center) in command of the new Continental Army. He was a humble man, but he accepted the post. He often used his own money to support the new army.

Colors had thirteen red and white alternating stripes, representing the thirteen united colonies. A small Union Jack (the British flag) filled the top left corner. Washington kept the Union Jack as a display of loyalty to King George and the British

Later that month, John took his turn at guard duty at the munitions site. A store of gunpowder accidentally ignited, and John received critical wounds from the blast. Fellow militiamen carried him home, but despite Betsy's best efforts to treat his wounds, John died. After less than two years of marriage, Betsy faced life and the war alone.

The Minutemen

Congress created the Continental Army and appointed General George Washington its commander in chief in 1775. Before that, armed citizens formed militias to protect their towns. Militiamen were usually between the ages of 16 and 60, but participation wasn't mandatory. Almost every colonial generation fought in some kind of armed conflict.

The minutemen were a special unit of the militia. Their main priority was a commitment to be ready for battle at a minute's notice. Most of them were young—25 years or younger. Officers handpicked these men from the ranks of the regular militia.

Both militia and minutemen provided their own guns and ammunition. They wore there own clothes into battle. They provided for themselves in every way while away from home, although the people in each town fed and housed them when possible. Most towns took their responsibilities to these men seriously. They would do without in order to feed the men.

The minutemen received special training that the regular militia didn't. As a result, they were the elite fighting force of their day. They were adept at Indian-style field scuffles—having abandoned the more formal battle line formation the British still used. They often painted themselves like Indians to intimidate their enemies.

Most of the minutemen were accurate hunters with their rifles, giving them an advantage over most of their opponents. The minutemen could fire and take cover before the British were even in range with their weapons. Most minutemen were sharpshooters.

In commemoration of the minutemen, Daniel Chester French constructed the well-known statue the *Concord Minuteman*. Dedicated in 1875, it stands at Old North Bridge in Concord, Massachusetts, where minutemen defeated the British one hundred years earlier. Inscribed on the base is the opening stanza of Ralph Waldo Emerson's 1837 *Concord Hymn*, with the immortal words, "the shot heard round the world."

The Concord Minuteman

Artist Henry Mosler painted this picture of General George Washington crossing the icy Delaware River on his way to Trenton, New Jersey. Several artists have captured this famous moment on canvas and almost all of them show General Washington standing. The truth is that he probably did not stand up on the trip over. Most likely, he sat like everyone else.

CHAPTER
4

To War and Beyond

The winter and spring of 1776 must have been bleak for Betsy. She struggled through her grief to keep her shop open. Facing the uncertainty of war, people didn't redecorate or refurbish their homes. Even when they did, Betsy had trouble finding quality materials. In between upholstery work, she sewed and repaired clothes for soldiers. That summer is when her legendary meeting with George Washington, George Ross, and Robert Morris is said to have taken place.

Shortly after Betsy supposedly completed her flag, the Congress declared independence. John Nixon, a colonel in the Pennsylvania militia, read the Declaration of Independence aloud to a cheering crowd on July 8.

The crowd lingered into the evening. They celebrated around bonfires in the street. They rang bells and shot off cannons. Fireworks lit the night sky. Whether Betsy had recovered enough from John's death to celebrate that day, we don't know. We do know that she was a Patriot, so it's easy to imagine her in the crowd, cheering and waving, despite her grief.

The jubilation didn't last long. British troops captured Long Island and Manhattan on August 27. Then they marched toward the new nation's capital, Philadelphia, Pennsylvania. General

Jean Ferris painted this famous picture of Betsy Ross showing George Washington the Stars and Stripes. Like all paintings of Betsy Ross, this one commemorates the legend but doesn't represent fact. There's nothing to suggest that Washington and other founding fathers returned to Betsy's home to see the completed flag.

Washington's quick thinking managed to stall the British for a while. He ordered all the boats on the Delaware River to sail to the Pennsylvania side of the river and to stay there. Doing so stranded the British troops in New Jersey.

The general's ingenious move bought Philadelphians a little time, but the British wouldn't stay stranded for long. As soon as the river froze solid, the British would just march across the ice to Philadelphia. Washington knew he had to act before the British did. On December 25, under cover of darkness, Washington and his troops crossed the Delaware River to surprise the British troops, who were still waiting for the river to freeze.

It took all night to ferry the men, horses, and gear around the large chunks of ice floating in the river. At daybreak, after marching almost ten miles, the Americans attacked the sleeping enemy. Washington captured men, equipment, food, clothes, and munitions.

About this time, Joseph Ashburn, a childhood friend of Betsy's, reentered her life. Family tradition says that Joseph had loved Betsy when they were children. He was now a privateer raiding enemy ships to supply the Patriots. He was the captain of the *Swallow*, and under the guise of ordering new flags, he paid Betsy a visit. Once the Delaware River froze, Joseph was stuck in Philadelphia for the winter. He spent a lot of his free time with Betsy, and eventually he won her heart.[1] They married on June 15, 1777.

By August, the British General Howe was marching toward Philadelphia with 228 ships and 19,000 men. Panicked citizens deserted the city. Patriots moved the Liberty Bell to Allentown, Pennsylvania. Washington marched his army of 11,000 through, and then out of, Philadelphia. Marching toward the British, he meant to engage them before they could reach the city.

Philadelphians heard the cannons and, by mid-September, they knew the worst—Washington had lost! Those who could fled the city.

The noise must have been deafening as all those soldiers marched into the city, with their cannons and stamping horses, to the steady beat of the many drum corps. Loyalists met and cheered the British troops. The army settled in and began evicting Patriot families from their homes.

Betsy continued to make flags. Most likely, she worked on them upstairs at night so that the British troops and Loyalists wouldn't see her. Joseph, as a privateer for the revolutionary traitors, wasn't safe in town. He waited on his ship across the river.

Washington's attempt to free Philadelphia came in October and quickly failed. His army retreated to Valley Forge for the winter, but he left Patriot patrols around Philadelphia to keep the British trapped inside the city. Washington's men froze and starved as they waited for spring.

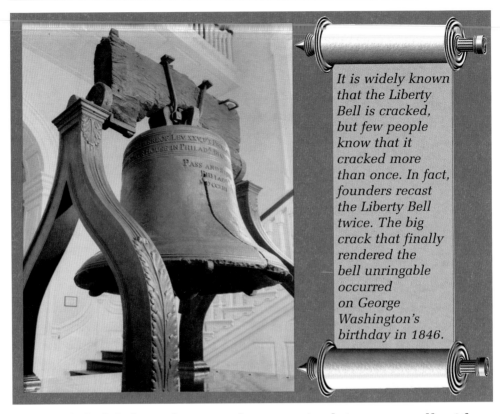

It is widely known that the Liberty Bell is cracked, but few people know that it cracked more than once. In fact, founders recast the Liberty Bell twice. The big crack that finally rendered the bell unringable occurred on George Washington's birthday in 1846.

In Philadelphia, the people weren't doing so well either. Firewood and food were scarce. When the firewood ran out, the British soldiers burned the Patriots' furniture. It was a fearsome winter.

In a surprise turn of events, King George ordered the British troops to leave Philadelphia. On June 18, 1778, British ships and troops left for New York.

The next few years were relatively quiet for Philadelphia. The war was raging across the colonies, but not in Philadelphia. Betsy and Joseph continued to support the war effort. Joseph continued his raids on enemy ships, capturing and carrying needed supplies to the Patriots. Betsy made flags and she added to their family. Zilla, Betsy and Joseph's first child, was born on September 15, 1779.

A year later, in October of 1780, Joseph took command of a new ship, the *Patty*, and sailed for the West Indies. He and Betsy,

who was pregnant again, expected the trip to last only a few weeks. They figured Joseph would be back long before the baby was born. But on February 25, 1781, a worried Betsy gave birth to her second daughter, Eliza, without Joseph at her side. He and his ship were missing.

We know very little about how Betsy spent the next several months. She kept her store opened, she took care of her girls, and she waited for news of Joseph. In the meantime, Cornwallis surrendered in late 1781, and the two sides began to exchange prisoners.

One of those prisoners was John Claypoole, the brother of Betsy's best friend, Susan Claypoole. He reached Philadelphia in early fall of 1782. One of the first things he did was to visit Betsy. Most likely, Betsy knew that John had been a prisoner of war and that he had returned to Philadelphia. Betsy was close to the entire Claypoole family.[2] Seeing John at her door must have been a powerfully sad moment for her. There was only one reason he would visit her so soon after returning home. Almost two years after seeing her husband off, Betsy received the news she had been dreading.

After a short exchange of greetings, John told Betsy his own story. The British captured his ship and eventually sent him to Limerick, Ireland. From there, a prison ship took him to the Old Mill Prison at Plymouth, which was the worst prison in England. There, he met Joseph. Joseph was very weak, having been a prisoner for over a year when John arrived. He continued to grow weaker and eventually fell sick in the damp, cold prison. On March 3, 1782, three months before John sailed for home, Joseph died. John stayed with his friend until the end.

The war for American independence had made Betsy a widow for the second time.

Sources are unclear on the exact date, but about this time, two-year-old Zilla died. Betsy must have been inconsolable for a while, having lost both her child and her husband at about the same time. In true Betsy fashion, though, she kept her shop open and continued to work. We don't know why, perhaps out of sense of chivalry and duty, but John continued to visit Betsy for several months Eventually, he returned to the sea and made several voyages to the West Indies.

Family tradition tells us that John would visit Betsy between voyages. The two missed each other while he was at sea. Eventually they admitted their feelings and they were married on May 8, 1783.

With a new wife and family to care for, John left the sea and joined Betsy in her upholstery business. She taught him everything she knew about the trade. John brought some skills of his own to the merger. As a boy, he had worked in his father's tanning shop. Together, the two produced upholstery and leather goods. Their business was successful, and they added five more girls to the family. One of them, Harriet, died in infancy.

The Claypooles lived well in postwar Philadelphia. Eventually, John went to work at the United States Custom House. Even though he made a good living there, Betsy kept the shop open and taught her girls the business. Betsy was sixty-five when John died on August 13, 1817. As before, she kept the shop open, but this time she had the help and support of her family.

Betsy continued to work in the shop for ten more years. Only when she lost her sight did she finally retire. At seventy-five, she turned the business over to her daughter Clarissa and her niece Margaret Boggs.[3]

At first, she lived in the country with Susannah Claypoole Satterthwaite, one of her daughters. A few years later, she returned to Philadelphia, where she lived with another daughter, Jane Claypoole Canby. Three years later, on January 30, 1836, Betsy died, surrounded by her children and grandchildren.[4] She was eighty-six years old.

Betsy's life was full. She survived a terrible war, had seven daughters, watched seven presidents lead the new nation, saw twelve states added to the Union, and ran her own successful business for fifty years.

Perhaps her most important accomplishment was her gift of the Stars and Stripes—if you're inclined to believe the legend. Betsy's flag would have had thirteen stars, one for each of the thirteen colonies. In 1836, when Betsy died, the flag had twenty-five stars.

American Revolution Prisoners of War

Betsy never knew that her second husband, Joseph Ashburn, had been a prisoner of war until months after his death.[5] If she had known, she might have sent him warm clothing, nonperishable food, and even medicine. Chances were those supplies would not have reached him, but she would've tried. Many families did.

During the Revolutionary War, both sides captured and kept prisoners instead of killing them outright. However, neither side felt obligated to provide for those prisoners. Rations were poor and medicine nonexistent. Each prisoner's unit provided food and supplies for their captured men, if they could. Prisoners could receive packages from home. They bought or exchanged food and clothing if they could.

The British were unable to hold occupied territory for very long. A few prisoner-of-war facilities were erected in New York, Philadelphia, and Charleston. Most of the time, British troops took their American prisoners with them when they retreated or moved.

Eventually, the British used captured or damaged ships as prisons. The conditions onboard were dreadful, and many prisoners died. Usually, they died of illness or exposure, complicated by malnutrition. Lack of food was the primary problem. If a prisoner got sick, his malnourished body couldn't fight off the disease, and he never recovered.

The Continental Army had a different system. They contracted with farmers to house and feed British prisoners. British prisoners helped work the farms in return for their room and board, which the farmers supplied. It was a good arrangement for everyone, including the prisoners. The farmer got the help he needed to keep the American troops fed. The British prisoners spent their captivity in somewhat humane conditions, compared to their counterparts in British prisons. It's unlikely that farmers supplied medicines or medical care for the prisoners. However, the prisoners did receive adequate food and shelter.

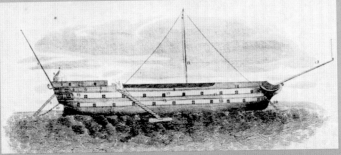

The "Old Jersey" Prison Ship

33

The flag on the top is called the Great
Union Flag. The American colonies adopted
that flag before declaring independence
from England. The canton in the left top
corner is the British flag, used to show that
the colonies were still subjects to England's
king. Traditional tells us that the canton
eventually morphed into the blue field with
white stars on the American flag (bottom)
that we know and honor today.

CHAPTER 5

Legend Meets Fact

On June 14, 1777, the newly established Congress of the American colonies adopted the following resolution:

Resolved, that the flag of the united states be 13 stripes alternated red and white, and the Union be 13 stars white in a blue field representing a new constellation.[1]

This resolution is where the official account of the origin of the Stars and Stripes begins and ends. Yet for over a century, schoolchildren have learned and loved the story of Betsy Ross. Historians argue that her story is fluff—the stuff of myth and legend. But then, most legends evolve from some kernel of truth.

Betsy's legend begins about a hundred years after the flag resolution, when William J. Canby, Betsy's grandson, shared a family story with the Historical Society of Pennsylvania. What had been only a family tale was about to change American history—whether it was true or not.

William Canby was eleven years old when Betsy Ross, his grandmother, died. He heard Betsy's story of how she had sewn the first Stars and Stripes for the rebelling colonies many times—straight from her. Clarissa, Betsy's daughter and William's aunt, asked William to write Betsy's story.

Later, he went to great lengths to verify his grandmother's story. The Secretary of State even granted Canby permission to examine the State Department archives. Canby found nothing to support his grandmother's story. In lieu of official documentation, Canby got more than a dozen affidavits from people who heard the story from Betsy or from one of her daughters.

George Preble included William's story in his second edition of *History of the Flag*. From there, the story made its way into schoolbooks across America, and eventually into history.

We know only a few things about Betsy: She was born and lived in Philadelphia; she was a Quaker until her marriage to John Ross; she was a Patriot; she was a seamstress and upholsterer; she lost two husbands to the war; she bore seven children, two of whom died in childhood; and she made flags. The rest of her story comes from family tradition and is not documented fact.

Most historians use the 1777 flag resolution to discredit Betsy's story. They insist that Betsy couldn't have sewn the Stars and Stripes flag a full year before Congress passed the flag resolution. It's a good argument, assuming that the physical flag came only after the resolution. There's no way to prove that a Stars and Stripes flag didn't (or did) exist before the resolution. If the committee truly acted in secret, they would've done so without an official flag resolution from the Congress.

Curiously, when Congress adopted and signed the Declaration of Independence, they appointed a committee to design an official seal. But there's no mention of a committee to design a national flag.[2] That omission leads to two possible conclusions: Either a design for a flag already existed, or the Congress hadn't yet considered a national flag. It's difficult to imagine that the Congress would've overlooked a national flag. Such a symbol would have boosted morale among the troops and the citizens.

The absence of any identity of who inserted the resolution or any discussion surrounding the resolution is also curious. Either there was no need for discussion or they simply left it out. Nor does the resolution give credit to anyone for the flag's design.

Another quarrel historians pick with Canby's story is whether General Washington was in Philadelphia the summer of 1776. A letter from John Hancock, dated June 3, 1776, seems to confirm that he was:

> I am extremely sorry it is not in my power to wait upon you in person to execute the command of Congress. But being deprived of this pleasure by a severe Fit of the gout . . .[3]

John Hancock was President of the Congress, and he was in Philadelphia at that time. Congress summoned Washington to Philadelphia late that spring to discuss his plans for the new army. Whether he also considered a flag for the new nation during those few weeks is a mystery—there's no evidence to suggest that he did so in any of his diaries, journals, or letters.

The subject of flags does appear in the postscript of a letter he wrote on May 28, 1776, to a Major General Putnam in New York: "I desire you'll speak to the several Colls [colonels] & hurry them to get their colours done."[4]

However, Washington is speaking about the regimental flags (colours), not a national flag. There are many similar references, as many regiments were eager to obtain flags. However, none of these known references specifically identifies the Stars and Stripes by name or by description. The most important issue in these references seems to be one of recognition—the regiments (and ships) needed flags that other Patriot regiments would recognize.

The only reference to Betsy's Stars and Stripes flag, outside of her family, comes from the niece of Roger Sherman. As a delegate to Congress, he helped draft, and he signed, the Declaration of Independence. His niece said:

> When a little later, George Washington designed and ordered the new flag to be made by Betsy Ross, nothing would satisfy Aunt Rebecca but to go and see it in the works, and there she had the privilege of sewing some of the stars on the very first flag of a Young Nation.[5]

The quote, while somewhat contemporary, isn't proof—it's just another story once removed from the principal players. Sherman was a delegate, so it is possible that he, and consequently his wife, knew of the committee's plans for a flag. It's entirely likely

John Hancock was the president of the Continental Congress. If he gave any thought to designing a flag for his new nation, there's no documentation to prove it.

that if the story is true, there was no congressional committee at all. The three Patriots may have acted on their own.

With no documentation to prove (or disprove) Canby's story, the next step would be to look for physical evidence of Betsy's flag. No one has ever turned up even a remnant of that first flag. Nor has anyone ever found the watercolor supposedly painted by William Barrett[6] at General Washington's special request—the painting that Betsy used as a guide.

There's no tradition of any regiment carrying the Stars and Stripes during the Revolutionary War. For the most part, most military units used custom colors—flags chosen by the individual regiments. More than a hundred years would pass before the army received authorization to carry the national flag.[7] This fact does not negate the legend, but it does make it harder to prove.

Traditionally, the first American flag, known as the Continental Colors, flew first on December 3, 1775. John Paul Jones claimed to have sailed under this new flag—raising it himself. After liberating Boston in January of 1776, we know that General Washington flew the Continental Colors, also known as the Great Union Flag. This was the first flag to represent the united colonies. It was the predecessor to the flag we know today as the Stars and Stripes. (John Paul Jones' claim is widely accepted, although we have only his retelling of the event as evidence.)

The Continental Colors had alternating red and white stripes. A small Union Jack (the British flag) graced the canton (the top left corner). Merging stripes that represented the colonies with the British Union Jack was a compromise that recognized the move toward self-government while still honoring England and her king. The flag was a stepping-stone to the real thing—a murmur of what was to come.

At this time, the colonists weren't demanding independence from England. They wanted the right to govern themselves; they didn't want total independence from England. A new flag wasn't appropriate yet. General Washington couldn't swear his loyalty to King George and then fly the flag of a new nation—even in battle. It was important at this point that the Patriots keep up the pretense of preferring reconciliation with England to war.

An early documented reference to the Stars and Stripes in battle comes from the diary of a British lieutenant named William Digby. On June 30, 1777, he wrote the following:

> . . . the 9th took their colours which were intended as a present to their Colonel, Lord Leganeer [*sic pro* Ligonier]. They were very handsome, a Flag of the United States, 13 Stripes, alternate red and white, in a blue field representing a new constellation.[8]

It is possible that a Stars and Stripes flag was present at Valley Forge the winter of 1777 and 1778. The Valley Forge Historical Society owns the flag, and contemporary experts have examined what's left of it. Thirteen white six-point stars in a horizontal pattern top the faded blue silk. Experts found that the flag is really a piece of another larger flag. It's easy to surmise that the flag originally came from a Stars and Stripes that simply no longer exists in its original condition, but there's no way to prove it.[9] The six-point stars aren't troublesome. Many people would've made flags, and some

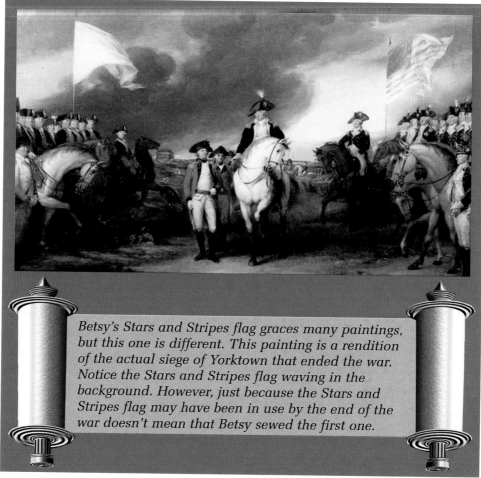

Betsy's Stars and Stripes flag graces many paintings, but this one is different. This painting is a rendition of the actual siege of Yorktown that ended the war. Notice the Stars and Stripes flag waving in the background. However, just because the Stars and Stripes flag may have been in use by the end of the war doesn't mean that Betsy sewed the first one.

would've preferred six-point stars. The resolution required thirteen stars, but it didn't specify the number of points for each star.

Colonial Williamsburg, Inc., owns a contemporary watercolor of the siege of Yorktown, where Cornwallis surrendered. The picture, painted by a British officer who was present during the battle, shows the Stars and Stripes (see above).[10] This, as a contemporary source, it probably one of the most convincing pieces of evidence that the Stars and Stripes was flown during the Revolutionary War. Unfortunately, there's no way to connect that flag, or any other Stars and Stripes flag, to Betsy Ross.

Congress took its last action on the flag on April 4, 1818. This resolution established the thirteen alternating red and white

stripes and the blue field with white stars. It also resolved to add a star for each state that joins the union.[11]

It is possible that General Washington and the flag committee designed the flag in secret and commissioned Betsy Ross to make it. If indeed they were acting in secrecy, there would be no official documentation. However, that doesn't explain why none of the committee members ever mentioned the flag later. Traditionally, George Washington was a humble man and seldom took credit for any of his deeds. This might explain his silence on the subject. Betsy didn't keep diaries, but we know she didn't remain silent on the subject of the Stars and Stripes flag within her family. She just didn't record the story in any contemporary trappings.

Perhaps Betsy or William simply lied. However, considering the affidavits Canby obtained from Betsy's contemporaries and children, it's hard to imagine that such a lie could have persisted for so long. Besides, Betsy Ross and William Canby both had a reputation of honesty and sincerity in their contemporary communities. Nothing in their known histories indicates that either might have lied.

Family members might have embellished the story with time. However, Canby obtained affidavits from Betsy's niece, Margaret Boggs, and two of Betsy's daughters. (Margaret lived with the family and worked in the shop with Betsy for many years.) All three women swore that Betsy told them the story from the time they were children. Each included a statement retelling the story in their own words with her affidavit. All three versions are similar.

No one knows who designed or created the first Stars and Stripes flag. Canby's story credits General Washington for designing it and Betsy Ross for bringing that design to life. The fact remains that no one has ever received official recognition or compensation for either task.

Regardless of the documented facts, Americans continue to support the Betsy Ross legend. In fact, most Americans don't even realize it is just a legend. Americans want to believe in Betsy Ross. Perhaps, Americans choose to believe in what Betsy Ross represents, with or without her flag—independence.

Commemorating Betsy Ross

    Birth of Our Nation's Flag is a portrait of Betsy Ross meeting the flag committee (above), painted by Charles H. Weisgerber. There are no portraits of Betsy Ross, so the artist used pictures of her granddaughters to come up with a composite. The Columbian Exposition in Chicago exhibited the painting in 1893.

    A few years later, in 1898, a group of over 20 people, including Charles Weisgerber, incorporated The American Flag House and Betsy Ross Memorial Association for the purpose of purchasing and preserving the house Betsy lived in when she would have sewn the flag (the house on Arch Street). The association raised money by selling ten-cent subscriptions, mostly to schoolchildren, to the house and association. Each contributor received a certificate of membership, a picture of the house, and a reproduction of *Birth of Our Nation's Flag*. This subscription drive did as much to spread Betsy's story as Canby had.

    Apparently, the artist took liberties with more than just Betsy's face. He also painted the stars in a circle. This arrangement adds to the mystery of the real Stars and Stripes and gives Canby critics something else to use to contradict Betsy's story. Eventually, the portrait's circular star pattern worked its way into the legend, even though there's nothing in Canby's traditional story to suggest Betsy Ross sewed the stars in a circle. However, that circle has come to represent Betsy Ross's Stars and Stripes. This circular pattern is misinformation and detracts from both sides of the issue.

    In 1952, to commemorate Betsy Ross's two-hundredth birthday, the United States government issued a stamp honoring her. The three-cent stamp shows Betsy holding a flag for the committee to review. As with Weisgerber's painting, people mistakenly use the stamp as evidence that the Betsy Ross story is fact.

Chapter Notes

Chapter 1   The Legend of Betsy Ross

1. "Five-Pointed Star in One Snip" (instructions) http://www.ush-istory.org/betsy/flagstar.html

2. Philadelphia Guild of Change Ringers, "Christ Church," http://www.phillyringers.com/christchurch/

3. "Christ Church, Philadelphia: A Brief Colonial History," http://www.christchurchphila.org/history.html

Chapter 2   A Colonial Quaker

1. Daniel J. Boorstin and Brooks Mather Kelly, with Ruth Frankel Boorstin, *A History of the United States* (Upper Saddle River, New Jersey: Pearson Prentice Hall, 2005), p. 64.

2. Robert Morris, *The Truth About the Betsy Ross Story* (Beach Haven, New Jersey: Wynnehaven Publishing Co., 1982), p. 23.

Chapter 3   Betsy and the Colonies Come of Age

1. Robert Morris, *The Truth About the Betsy Ross Story* (Beach Haven, New Jersey: Wynnehaven Publishing Co., 1982), p. 6.

2. Ibid., p. 8.

Chapter 4   To War and Beyond

1. Robert Morris, *The Truth About the Betsy Ross Story* (Beach Haven, New Jersey: Wynnehaven Publishing Co., 1982), p. 98.

2. Ibid., p. 105.

3. Ibid., p. 117.

4. Ibid., p. 119.

5. Ibid., pp. 103–104.

Chapter 5   Legend Meets Fact

1. Thomas Parrish, *The American Flag* (New York: Simon and Schuster, 1973), p. 61.

2. Lloyd Balderston, Ph.D, and George Canby, *The Evolution of the American Flag* (Philadelphia: Ferris & Leach, 1909), pp. 49–50.

3. Ibid., pp. 51–52.

4. William Furlong and Byron McCandless, *So Proudly We Hail: The History of the United States Flag* (Washington, D.C.: Smithsonian Institution Press, 1981), p. 116.

5. Cokie Roberts, *Founding Mothers: The Women Who Raised Our Nation* (New York: HarperCollins Publishers, Inc., 2004), p. 131.

6. Balderston and Canby, p. 117.

7. Albert I. Mayer, *The Story of Old Glory* (Chicago: Childrens Press, 1970), p. 18.

8. Balderston and Canby, pp. 62–63.

9. Furlong and McCandless, pp. 119–120.

10. Mayer, p. 21.

11. Devereaux D. Cannon, Jr., *The Flags of the Union* (Gretna, LA: Pelican Publishing Company, 1994), p. 21.

Chronology

1752	Elizabeth "Betsy" Griscom is born on January 1 in Philadelphia, Pennsylvania.
1764	Betsy begins her apprenticeship as an upholsterer.
1773	Betsy elopes with John Ross.
1774	Betsy's Quaker community reads her out of Meeting for marrying a non-Quaker. She and John open their own upholstery business.
1775	Betsy joins The Fighting Quakers.
1776	John Ross dies from wounds sustained from an explosion.
	A special Congressional committee visits Betsy and asks her to make a flag.
1777	Betsy marries Joseph Ashburn. He leaves to fight the war.
1779	Their first child, Zilla, is born on September 15.
1781	Their second daughter, Eliza, is born on February 25.
1782	Betsy learns from John Claypoole that her husband died in an English prison. Zilla dies.
1783	Betsy marries John Claypoole.
1784	Betsy joins the Society of Free Quakers.
1785	Betsy and John's first child, Clarissa, is born on April 3.
1786	Betsy gives birth to Susannah.
1789	Betsy gives birth to Rachel.
1792	Betsy gives birth to Jane.
1795	Betsy gives birth to Harriet on December 20.
1817	John Claypoole dies.
1827	Betsy retires from her upholstery business.
1836	Betsy dies on January 30.

Timeline in History

1682	Quaker William Penn founds the Pennsylvania colony.
1752	Patriots hang the Liberty Bell in the Philadelphia State House, now known as Independence Hall.
1774	The First Continental Congress meets in Carpenters' Hall, which Betsy Ross's father helped to build.
1775	Delegates to the Second Continental Congress appoint George Washington as the commander in chief to the new Continental Army on June 15.
1776	Congress adopts the Declaration of Independence.
1777	Congress passes the Flag Resolution on June 14. The British occupy Philadelphia.
1778	The Stars and Stripes receives its first foreign salute on February 14 when the admiral of the French fleet exchanges gun salutes with John Paul Jones, aboard the *Ranger*. The *Drake*, a British ship, surrenders to John Paul Jones, who is flying the Stars and Stripes—the flag's first naval conquest.
1781	General George Washington defeats Lord Cornwallis at Yorktown.
1783	The Revolutionary War officially ends.
1789	George Washington becomes the first president of the United States.
1790	The *Columbia*, a merchant ship, returns from a 42,000-mile voyage—completing the first around-the-world trip of any ship flying the American flag (August 10).
1804–1806	Lewis and Clark carry the American flag across the continent to the Pacific Ocean.
1812	The War of 1812 is fought against Great Britain.
1870	Betsy Ross's grandson, William Canby, tells her story to the Historical Society of Pennsylvania.
1937	All eight rooms of the Betsy Ross House on Arch Street in Philadelphia are open to the public.

Further Reading

For Young Adults

DeBarr, Candice M., and Jack A. Bonkowske. *Saga of the American Flag*. Tucson, Arizona: Harbinger House, Inc., 1990.

DePauw, Linda Grant. *Founding Mothers: Women of America in the Revolutionary Era*. New York: Houghton Mifflin Company, 1975.

Essenberger, David. *Flags of the U.S.A.* New York: Thomas Y. Crowell Company, 1959.

Mayer, Albert I. *The Story of Old Glory*. Chicago: Childrens Press, 1970.

Quaife, Milo M., Melvin J. Weig, and Roy E. Appleman. *The History of the United States Flag*. New York: Harper & Row, Publisher, 1961.

Roop, Peter, and Connie Roop. *Betsy Ross*. Chicago: Scholastic, Inc., 2001.

Works Consulted

Balderston, Lloyd, Ph.D., from materials collected by George Canby. *The Evolution of the American Flag*. Philadelphia: Ferris & Leach, 1909.

Boorstin, Daniel J., and Brooks Mather Kelly, with Ruth Frankel Boorstin. *A History of the United States* Upper Saddle River, New Jersey: Pearson Prentice Hall, 2005.

Cannon, Devereaux D. *The Flags of the Union*. Gretna, Louisiana: Pelican Publishing Company, 1994.

Furlong, William Rea, and Bryon McCandless. *So Proudly We Hail: The History of the United States Flag*. Washington, D.C.:
Smithsonian Institution Press, 1981.

Morris, Robert. *The Truth About the Betsy Ross Story*. Beach Haven, New Jersey: Wynnehaven Publishing Co., 1982.

Parrish, Thomas. *The American Flag*. New York: Simon and Schuster, 1973.

Roberts, Cokie. *Founding Mothers: The Women Who Raised Our Nation*. New York: HarperCollins Publishers, Inc., 2004.

On the Internet

Flag Picture Gallery
http://www.ushistory.org/betsy/flagpics.html

The Betsy Ross House
http://www.betsyrosshouse.org

The Flag of the United States of America
http://www.usflag.org/index.html

The Historical Society of Pennsylvania
http://www.hsp.org/

"The History of the Flag of the United States," by William Canby
http://www.ushistory.org/Betsy/more/canby.htm

Kashatus, William C. "Seamstress for a Revolution."
http://onlote.more.gov/aav/Archive/2005/Jun/07-729209.html

The Middle Colonies
http://www.kidinfo.com/American_History/Colonization_Mid_Colonies.html

The Religious Society of Friends
http://www.quaker.org

United States Flag
http://www.uen.org/utahlink/activities/view_activity.cgi?activity_id=3471

Glossary

affidavit (aa-fih-DAY-vit)
Sworn and signed testimony, usually made before a judge.

boycott (BOY-kot)
To refuse to buy or support a particular product or brand.

canton (KAN-tun)
The top left corner of a flag.

delegate (DEH-leh-gut)
A representative to a conference or convention.

Loyalists (LOY-uh-lists)
People who supported the King of England and were against independence for the American colonies.

militia (muh-LIH-shuh)
Armed citizens banding together to fight a common enemy.

minutemen (MIH-nut-men)
Special militiamen who were prepared to be ready to fight the British at a "minute's" notice.

pacifist (PAA-suh-fist)
A person who rejects violence or force.

Patriot (PAY-tree-ut)
A colonist who wanted American independence.

pound (POWND)
A British unit of money.

privateer (pry-vuh-TEER)
A merchant ship that captured supplies from the enemy.

segregate (SEH-grih-gayt)
To separate or divide by some attribute or quality, such as race or religion.

stocks (STOKS)
A wooden frame on a post with holes for the head and hands in which those guilty of minor offenses are locked as punishment.

stomacher (STUH-mih-kur)
A heavily embroidered or jeweled garment formerly worn over the chest and stomach by women.

tithing (TYTH-ing)
The Biblical commandment to give one-tenth of one's income to the church.

Index